UP CLOSE

SHARKS

LYNN GIBBONS & CHRIS COODE

W

Published in 2007 by Franklin Watts
Reprinted in 2010

Copyright © 2007 Arcturus Publishing Limited

Franklin Watts
338 Euston Road
London NW1 3BH

Franklin Watts Australia
Level 17/207 Kent Street
Sydney, NSW 2000

Authors: Lynn Gibbons and Chris Coode
Editor (new edition): Ella Fern
Designers (new edition): Steve West, Steve Flight

Picture credits: BBC: 4, 5 top left, 6 top left, 9 top left, 11, 23, back cover; Jamie Oliver: 20 top; Oxford Scientific: front cover, title page, 2, 5 center right, 6 bottom right, 7, 9 bottom right, 10, 13 bottom, 14, 15, 17, 18 top, 19 top, 21; Planet Earth: 3, 12 top, bottom, 16 top, bottom, 18 bottom, 20 bottom; Science Photo Library: 8, 13 top, 19 bottom.

A CIP catalogue record for this book is available from the British Library

Dewey number: 597.3

ISBN: 978-1-4451-0131-6
SL000943EN

Printed in China

Franklin Watts is a division of Hachette Children's Books, an Hachette UK Company
www.hachette.co.uk.

Contents

Masters of the

S hark. The very name can strike terror into many people's hearts. But sharks deserve much more than our fear. They also deserve our admiration and respect. These expert ocean hunters (predators) have been around for over 450 million years!

BONELESS
Sharks' skeletons are not made of bone, but a tough, bendable material called *cartilage*.

Deep

Our word "shark" comes from the German word *Schurke,* which means "greedy parasite" or "scoundrel."

COUSINS

Although there is little family resemblance, the shark's closest relatives are rays and skates.

Sharks have livers full of oil, which is lighter than water. This helps them to stay buoyant while swimming.

THAT'S ROUGH

A shark's body is covered in tiny, toothlike scales called *denticles.* These make their skin feel rough, like sandpaper.

5

EYE GUARD
Some sharks have a special eyelid that covers the eye to protect it when they attack their prey.

SWIFT
Sharks have a torpedo-shaped body. This allows them to glide quickly though the water.

S harks are the most successful predators in the ocean. They have a great sense of smell and their hearing is top notch. A shark can also pick up on vibrations in the water, so it can "feel" something without even touching it.

ELECTRIC
Sharks have electrical *sensors* on their noses that help them to pinpoint the exact location of their prey with amazing accuracy.

You With

Sharks can smell blood in the water from miles away.

Scientists aren't sure how sharks find their way around the ocean without getting lost. They think sharks may use their special "electro-sense" like a compass.

Better to Eat You With

The dinner menu is quite similar for most kinds of sharks. They prefer smaller fish (including other sharks) and squid. Sharks often prey on sick or wounded animals, since they are easier to catch.

APPETIZER

Great white sharks have several rows of teeth to bite with. They can digest almost anything. A great white's teeth are jagged, so a tasty leg wouldn't pose any problem at all.

DENTAL CARE

Every time a shark eats, some of its teeth either break or fall out. Luckily, every time a tooth falls out, a new one takes its place.

TAKE A BITE

The cookie-cutter shark has a round mouth that is specially designed to take biscuit-sized bites out of larger animals like whales and dolphins.

FILTERS

Huge sharks like the whale shark and the megamouth have mouths that act like giant strainers. They filter *plankton* out of the water.

Tiger sharks' stomachs were found to contain tin cans, license plates and an alarm clock!

A shark's jaws are not connected to its skull. This means it can open its mouth REALLY wide. Then it snaps its powerful jaws shut, just like a trap.

The Good, the Bad, and the Ugly

There are more than 375 species of sharks. Whale sharks can grow more than 15 metres long. Pygmy sharks are less than 15 centimetres long and can fit in the palm of your hand.

FUNNY FACE

Hammerhead sharks have strange, T-shaped heads. Their eyes are on either side of their heads, so they have excellent all-around vision.

The fastest shark is the shortfin mako, which can swim up to 48 kph in short bursts.

HORNSHARK

The hornshark has two sharp spines that stick out from its *dorsal* fins.

SOFT TOUCH

This spotted wobbegong is also called a carpet shark. It has a mottled skin like the pattern on a carpet.

CAMOUFLAGE

Spots and blotches help sharks to blend in with plants and rocks on the seafloor.

SPOTS OR STRIPES?

Baby zebra sharks have black and yellow stripes. As they grow, the markings change into pale brown spots.

Many sharks are dark on top and pale underneath. Their colouring blends in with the dark waters below and the sunlit waters above.

The Heavyweights

W ho are the giants of the shark world? The most feared *predator* is the great white. The whale shark, known as the "gentle giant", is the largest shark of all.

GREAT WHITE

Size: It is about 6 metres long and weighs over 2 tonnes.

Diet: The great white has teeth that are 5 centimetres long. It eats fish and sea *mammals* like seals and sea lions.

WHALE SHARK

Size: The whale shark is the largest shark in the world. It measures over 14 metres long and weighs more than 13 tonnes.

Diet: Plankton. The shark takes in huge mouthfuls of water. The lining in its throat is like a sieve, trapping the plankton for the shark to swallow.

JAWS—TRUTH XPOSED!

The film *Jaws* made many people afraid to go into the water. But the great white shark they filmed was a model with with extra teeth. It would sink if it were real.

TINY TEETH

The whale shark's mouth is lined with thousands of tiny teeth. Biologists aren't sure what they use their teeth for.

Human-Infested Waters

S hark attacks on humans are extremely rare. There are about 50 attacks reported each year, and only two or three kill people. The sharks most likely to attack humans are the tiger, bull, great white, and oceanic whitetip shark.

Coconuts injure more people than sharks!

MISTAKE
A shark can mistake a diver for a seal or a sea turtle.

HUMAN ATTACK!

Every year, 200 million sharks are killed by humans. They are fished for their meat, skin, teeth, oil, and just for fun.

POLLUTION

Sharks are also threatened by pollution. Chemicals in the water kill the fish they eat. Oil spills destroy their breeding grounds.

Chances are you will never be attacked by a shark. But it's a good idea not to swim where sharks have been seen. Remember, the ocean is their home—you are just a visitor.

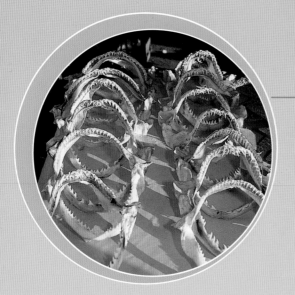

TACKY SOUVENIRS

Sharks are killed for their jaws as well, which are removed and sold as souvenirs.

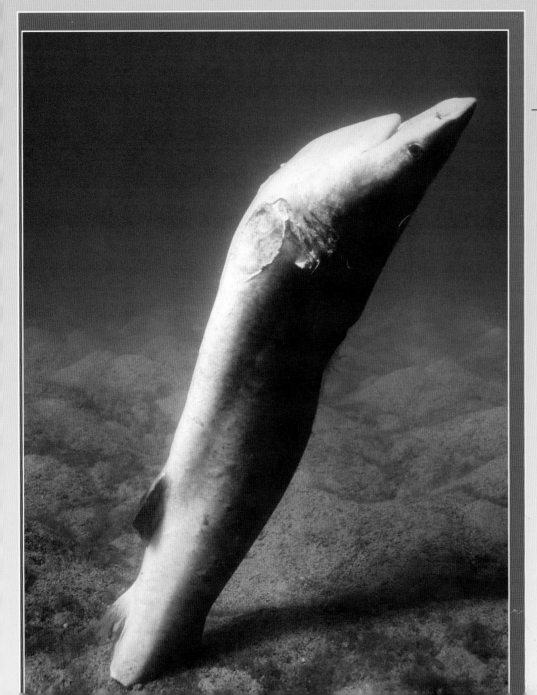

WASTE

Many sharks are accidentally caught and killed in nets meant for other fish. Others, like this one, are caught for their fins. The rest of the body is thrown back into the sea to rot.

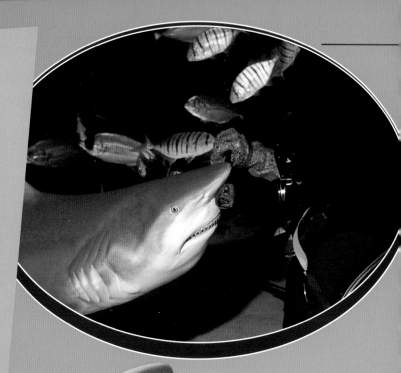

So many sharks are killed each year that several kinds are in big trouble. They are classified as threatened species, which means they could die out altogether. If this happens, all of ocean life would suffer.

HEALTH SHARKS

Sharks hardly ever get ill. Finding out why sharks are so healthy could help us stay well too.

SPIRITS

Some Pacific Islanders believe sharks are the spirits of their dead ancestors.

Sharks

At aquariums, visitors can a get a great view of live sharks. Seeing sharks up close helps us understand that sharks are worth far more alive than dead.

— ACTION

The more we know about sharks, the more we can do to help save them. *Conservation groups* have set up underwater nature reserves where sharks can live in safety.

We must help to save the sharks by respecting them.

Glossary

Camouflage
The way animals blend into their surroundings, usually so that predators can't see them.

Cartilage
Tough, fibrous and elastic tissue. Sharks' skeletons are made of cartilage. It is also found in human ears and noses.

Conservation group
A group of conservationists—people who work to conserve species and natural habitats that are under threat.

Denticles
Tiny tooth-like scales that cover a shark.

Dorsal
Relating to the back e.g., dorsal fin.

Mammal
An animal that is warm-blooded and gives birth to live young. Sea mammals are mammals that live in the sea, like seals.

Plankton
Tiny organisms (plants or animals) that live at the surface of the water.

Predator
An animal (a carnivore) that hunts and eats other animals.

Sensor
Something that receives a signal and responds to it.

Further Reading

The Best Book of Sharks
Claire Llewellyn, Kingfisher, 2005

The Everything Kids' Shark Book
Kathi Wagner and Obe Wagner, Adams
Media, 2005

**Sharkabet: A Sea of Sharks from
A to Z**
Ray Troll, Westwinds Press, 2002

Sharks
Jonathan Sheik-Miller, Usborne
(Discovery series), 2000

Sharks
Miranda Macquitty, Dorling Kindersley
(Eyewitness series), 1992

Index